A GIFT FOR:_____

FROM:_____

For Mary Ann Laskoski, beloved aunt and constant inspiration. —LH

Random Acts of Awesome

Design: Cindy Butler

Typography: Aracne Condensed, Avenir, Minion Pro

Image Credits:
Mother Teresa: Suma Iyer. Walter Cronkite: Nationaal Archief, the Dutch National Archives. Roald Dahl: Carl Van Vechten Photographs collection at the Library of Congress. Bill Nye, Barack Obama, Neil deGrasse Tyson, Ernest Hemingway, Mozart, and Rosa Parks wikimedia.comThe Cowardly Lion, used with permission by Charles Santore and Cider Mill Press Book Publishers, from *The Wizard of Oz*. Arnold Schwarzenegger, Chuck Norris, Steven Spielberg, Peter Dinklage used under official license from alamy.com
All other photos used under official license from shutterstock.com

ISBN: 978-1-63059-748-1
BOK1089

Made in China
1217

RANDOM ACTS OF AWESOME
25 WORDS TO INSPIRE YOU TO CHANGE THE WORLD

By Lou Harry

TABLE OF CONTENTS

GENEROUS

Think you have to have it all to be generous? Think again. Perhaps it's more useful and, well, generous, to think of generosity in broader terms. Yes, it's wonderful when philanthropists with a net worth in the billions funnel part of their fortune into endowing hospital wings or funding new centers for the arts. But the person on a limited income who helps out when they see someone a few dollars short at the supermarket or the volunteer who finds a few hours a week to help out at a local nursing home is being no less generous. Think of generosity as simply giving without consideration for the potential benefits to your own prestige, power, or bottom line. Choosing to be generous in some way, big or small, is choosing to transcend your own needs. One wonderful side effect? We come to understand that the people around us are just as important as we are.

PROFILE IN GENEROSITY:

Ascending to the top of the list of richest people in the world thanks to the success of his company, Microsoft, Bill Gates eventually transformed himself from one of the most successful businesspeople in history to one of the most charitable people in the world. Gates and his wife formed the Bill & Melinda Gates Foundation in 2000, and that foundation has gone on to distribute more than $41 billion in grants to global health programs, U.S. education, emergency relief agencies, and more. "Is the rich world aware of how four billion of the six billion live?" Gates asked. "If we were aware, we would want to help out, we'd want to get involved."

For a smaller-scale example, consider the young woman in Carmel, IN, who earned national attention in 2017 when she turned her canceled $30,000 wedding reception into a party for the homeless. Her nonrefundable contract specified dinner for 170 guests. Rather than call off the affair when her engagement was broken off, she contacted local homeless shelters. Inspired by her act of generosity, local businesses and residents donated dresses, suits, and more. And members of the wedding party joined her in welcoming the new guests.

"OBVIOUSLY, YOU WOULD GIVE YOUR LIFE FOR YOUR CHILDREN, OR GIVE THEM THE LAST BISCUIT ON THE PLATE. BUT TO ME, THE TRICK IN LIFE IS TO TAKE THAT SENSE OF GENEROSITY BETWEEN KIN, MAKE IT APPLY TO THE EXTENDED FAMILY AND TO YOUR NEIGHBOR, YOUR VILLAGE, AND BEYOND."

–PLAYWRIGHT TOM STOPPARD

COURAGE

Remember the Cowardly Lion in *The Wizard of Oz*? He journeyed far from his home in search of courage and, like his friends, found that he had the trait he was seeking all along. His problem? He assumed that courage meant having no fear. His courage, though, came from moving forward in spite of his fears and finding a way to stand strong when needed. Sure, that not-too-ferocious feline is fictional. But we've got a piece of him within us. As the song from the Broadway Oz-adaptation *The Wiz* tells us, "Be a lion/ In your own way."

PROFILE IN COURAGE:

The ultimate test of courage is putting your own life on the line. And Witold Pilecki did that not just in a moment, but over several years. Pilecki volunteered to be imprisoned at Auschwitz in order to gather the first comprehensive Allied intelligence reports on the Nazi atrocities there. The Polish soldier spent nearly two-and-a-half years at Auschwitz before escaping with valuable information. And his sacrifices didn't end there. A founder of the Secret Polish Army, he fought in the Warsaw uprising and remained loyal to the exiled Polish government that was based in London. Pilecki continued to fight for freedom until he was captured, tortured, and executed by Soviet forces in 1948.

"ALL MEN ARE FRIGHTENED. THE MORE INTELLIGENT THEY ARE, THE MORE THEY ARE FRIGHTENED. THE COURAGEOUS MAN IS THE MAN WHO FORCES HIMSELF, IN SPITE OF HIS FEAR, TO CARRY ON."

— GENERAL GEORGE S. PATTON, JR.

INSPIRE

Inspiration is an almost magical thing that can happen without the inspirer even knowing it. Being a role model, projecting positivity, and being open and honest about struggles can cause inspiration to ripple across space and time, leading to something wonderful. Hardly an awards show goes by without some winner—often many—thanking an inspiring high school choir or drama teacher. Top athletes praise the coaches who inspired them during their young lives. But inspiration isn't just for the young. Who wouldn't be inspired by the woman in her 60s who, when diagnosed with cancer, decided to take piano lessons for the first time in her life?

PROFILE IN INSPIRATION:

Nobody likes rejection. And when you face dozens of rejections, it's easy to give up. Factor in the other challenges of life—in this case, a divorce and being on government aid—and you could totally understand someone throwing in the towel on their dream. But J.K. Rowling didn't. She continued to submit her writing to publishers, even hand-typing her manuscripts because she couldn't afford a computer. Then, *voilà*, the first *Harry Potter* novel was published. Rowling is now one of the wealthiest women in England. Her life—and the world of entertainment—hasn't been the same since.

CAPTIVATE

The ability to hold the attention of others—whether that's while making a business presentation, chiming in at a PTA meeting, or keeping passengers engaged during a long road trip—is a valuable trait. Yes, you can captivate with beauty. And you can captivate with excellence in sports or the arts. But you can also captivate simply by being someone worth listening to.

FORGIVE

If you find it difficult to forgive common slights (and who doesn't?), imagine the strength and fortitude summoned by those who have lost loved ones at the hands of others but still are able to forgive. Such stories of forgiveness, while not common, are numerous. And we can take inspiration from those extreme cases as we try to forgive those who have wronged us. And forgiveness is therapeutic: Clinging to the past can be more damaging for you than the person who wronged you.

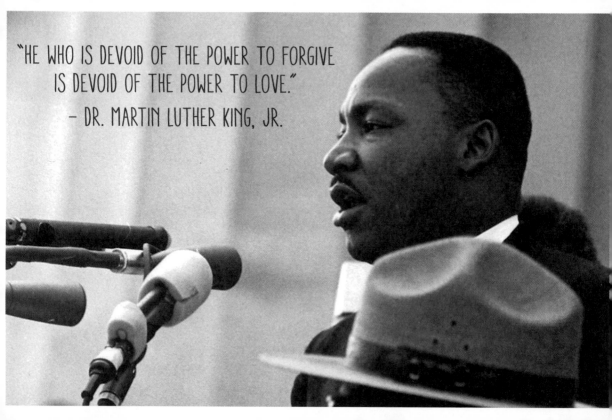

PROFILE IN FORGIVENESS:

Even as he suffered through years in prison while leading the struggle to free India from British rule, revenge wasn't in Mahatma Gandhi's heart. He spent his life proving both the strength of non-violence and the human capacity for forgiveness. According to UPI, Gandhi even put his hand to his forehead in a gesture of forgiveness to his assassin. " "The weak can never forgive," he said. "Forgiveness is the attribute of the strong."

BRAVE

Bravery isn't the same as a lack of fear. Instead, it's facing a dangerous challenge in spite of that fear. You can find obvious examples in the military and public service— police, firefighters, etc., who risk their lives as a matter of course. But there's bravery to be found all over, from astronauts and prison guards to ordinary citizens who find themselves in extraordinarily dangerous circumstances.

→ IT'S A FACT: ←

ADMIRE THE COURAGE OF WINDOW WASHERS? YOU SHOULD. THOSE
WHO HELD THAT JOB WERE THE MOST LIKELY TO BE RECOGNIZED FOR
BRAVERY WHEN THEY BECAME SOLDIERS DURING WORLD WAR I.

PROFILE IN BRAVERY:

Just a tired woman? Nope. "The only tired I was," said Rosa Parks, "was tired of giving in." Few in America are unaware of the woman who became a legend in the Civil Rights Movement for refusing to give up her seat on a Montgomery, Alabama, bus in 1955. But Parks' act wasn't an isolated incident or a spur-of-the-moment decision. She had a history of activism before and after the incident, having been actively involved in the NAACP for a decade. Even after she and her husband lost their jobs due to the boycott and moved to Detroit, they continued their fight against discrimination.

CARE

Not only do other people in the world matter, it is our duty to make the world better for them when we can. That's the essence of caring. While thoughtfulness is the starting point, action is where true caring comes through. For some, that means a profession centered on caring—nursing, for instance. For others, it means checking in on neighbors or volunteering at shelters. It can mean doing something personally or donating to a cause that's able to achieve what an individual can't.

PROFILE IN CARING:

Few in history have been as synonymous with the word caring as Mother Teresa. A missionary from the age of 18, she was inspired to serve the poorest of the poor while on a train ride in India and eventually created the Missionaries of Charity. Caring for the sick and the dying, washing the sores of children, and meeting needs wherever she found them, Mother Teresa soon attracted other sisters, who she dispatched to other areas of India ... then to Venezuela ... and then to the former Soviet Union and elsewhere. While she was honored with a Nobel Peace Prize in 1979, she never lost sight of her mission: Caring for those who needed it the most. By the time of her death, there were about 4,000 members of Mother Teresa's sisters, doing remarkable work in 123 countries.

When we grasp, deeply, the experiences of another person—when we put ourselves in their shoes and minimize our own agendas—we forge a deeper connection with all mankind. A cousin of caring, empathy implies that we understand the feelings of another to the point where their pain is practically our pain, and their struggles become ours. Empathy can also provide motivation—sometimes just knowing that someone truly empathizes with our challenges makes a world of difference.

IT'S A FACT:

WHILE STORIES ABOUND, THERE'S NO EVIDENCE THAT TWINS ACTUALLY FEEL EACH OTHER'S PAIN IN A SUPERNATURAL WAY. HOWEVER, EMPATHY CAN LEAD A PERSON TO IMAGINE THAT THEY ARE EXPERIENCING THE SAME SYMPTOMS AS ANOTHER.

"MAYBE PART OF OUR FORMAL EDUCATION SHOULD BE TRAINING IN EMPATHY. IMAGINE HOW DIFFERENT THE WORLD WOULD BE IF, IN FACT, THAT WERE 'READING, WRITING, ARITHMETIC, EMPATHY.' "

—SCIENTIST NEIL DEGRASSE TYSON

(PICTURED FROM LEFT TO RIGHT: BILL NYE, FORMER PRESIDENT BARACK OBAMA, AND TYSON)

DRIVE

Motivating can mean encouraging a student to aim higher, convincing a nursing home resident to participate in social activities, helping someone who is down on their luck get back in the game, taking on a mentorship role at work, or (gently or not) pushing people to be their best selves. Science tells us that a body at rest tends to stay at rest. Which is why people who can motivate others are to be cherished. And remember this: Any basketball coach will tell you it is just as important to be there for the assist as it is to score the basket.

PROFILE IN DRIVE:

Legendary coach and athletic director Homer Rice transformed an unremarkable program at Georgia Tech into a sports powerhouse. Not only did its football team become national champions, but the baseball team made it to a pair of College World Series, the basketball team reached a Final Four, and the women's basketball team won a WNIT title. And that does not account for the individual achievements of Techsters, which include a trio of Olympic gold medals in track and field. Rice's ability to motivate players was visible early in his career. In 1950, he not only led the high school team he coached to an unbeaten season, he did the same with a prison team he coached. His attitude:

"YOU CAN MOTIVATE BY FEAR, AND YOU CAN MOTIVATE BY REWARD. BUT BOTH THOSE METHODS ARE ONLY TEMPORARY. THE ONLY LASTING THING IS SELF MOTIVATION."

→→ **IT'S A FACT:** ←←

STUDIES HAVE SHOWN THAT FINANCIAL INCENTIVES CAN ACTUALLY SLOW DOWN TASKS THAT REQUIRE CREATIVE PROBLEM-SOLVING. PURPOSE, AUTONOMY, AND MASTERY CAN BE STRONGER INCENTIVES THAN FINANCIAL GAIN.

"SOMETIMES THE THINGS WE WANT MOST ARE THE HARDEST TO GET. THAT MEANS YOU NEED TO BE EVEN MORE DETERMINED TO SUCCEED. THAT'S WHAT IT TAKES TO BE A WINNER. YOU HAVE TO WANT IT BAD ENOUGH TO STICK WITH IT NO MATTER HOW TOUGH THINGS GET."

-ACTOR CHUCK NORRIS

TRANSFORM

No, this has nothing to do with those robots that turn into vehicles. Well, maybe it does. Starting with one thing and then shaping it so that it becomes another is a valuable and important skill. It involves being able to anticipate challenges and deal with those you can't. It involves bringing experience and knowledge to the table, but also requires you to be open to the lessons encountered along the way. And it can lead to a better company, a better neighborhood, a better country, and a better you.

PROFILE IN TRANSFORMATION:

It would be difficult to find a biography with more transformational moments than that of Arnold Schwarzenegger. How many Austrians become governors in another country, let alone hugely successful film stars? Born in Austria, Schwarzenegger first garnered attention as a bodybuilder, winning Mr. Olympia seven times once he moved to the U.S. After adding English classes to his training regimen, Schwarzenegger found small acting roles…which led to bigger acting roles…which led to superstar status. Then, with no record of holding public office, he ran for Governor of California—and won. If it wasn't for a Constitutional requirement that presidents must be born in the U.S., he most likely would have run for his adopted homeland's highest office.

RIGHTEOUS

For many, the word righteous brings to mind Atticus Finch, the protagonist in *To Kill a Mockingbird* who stands up to the prejudices of an entire community. And, while it is easy to see the righteous as excessively stubborn, having solid ethics and believing in core truths is ultimately the best way to serve one's community. The truly righteous person sees that the world can be a better place and understands that they need to be a part of that process.

PROFILE IN RIGHTEOUSNESS:

It's easy to believe that corporations are all about maximizing profits for shareholders and owners, often at the expense of hardworking employees. But Dan Price, CEO of Gravity Payments, drew the attention of the media—and fellow business leaders—when he implemented a dramatic salary restructuring plan for his employees and himself. Not only did Price raise the minimum salary for his staffers to $70,000, he also cut his own seven-figure salary to that amount. The move impacted about 70 employees. For some staffers, it meant doubling their income. "There is a moral imperative that comes with leadership to do what's right to those that you are leading and those you have made promises to," Price said.

"WE HAVE TO BE VERY CAREFUL ABOUT HOW WE AS A SPECIES USE OUR GENIUS. I THINK WE NEED TO TAKE RESPONSIBILITY FOR THE THINGS WE PUT ON THIS PLANET, AND ALSO TAKE RESPONSIBILITY FOR THE THINGS WE TAKE OFF THE PLANET. WE NEED TO HAVE LIMITERS ON HOW FAR WE ALLOW OURSELVES TO GO—ETHICAL, MORAL LIMITERS."
— DIRECTOR STEVEN SPIELBERG

TRUST

Grandparents know the joy of being entrusted with their children's children, even if only for a night. Employees know the empowerment that comes from a boss's faith in them. Being trusted and knowing you have people you can trust can make a big difference in your life. In a world with more than its share of lies and betrayals, it's important to not just surround yourself with people you trust, but also to be a person who can be trusted. Everything—from marriages to international peace treaties—depends on it.

PROFILE IN TRUST:

When it comes to trustworthiness and sincerity, people still speak reverentially of late newscaster Walter Cronkite, who headlined the CBS Evening News for 19 years. Even though he went off the air in 1981, his reputation as "the most trusted man in America" remains long after his death, standing in stark contrast to the public's skeptical view of TV news today. His steady handling of events during the turbulent 1960s and 1970s cemented his reputation for calm delivery of the news. In response to Cronkite's death, actor George Clooney said "His legacy will be one of the great legacies of great Americans ... Not just to generations before him but to generations coming up. That's probably good that there will never be a most trusted man in America again, because if we're not lucky enough to get Walter Cronkite, then we might be in a lot of trouble."

"BETTER TO TRUST THE MAN WHO IS FREQUENTLY IN ERROR THAN THE ONE WHO IS NEVER IN DOUBT."

– JOURNALIST ERIC SEVAREID

GRACE

The magic of a ballet performance isn't just the remarkable athleticism displayed in the leaps and twists. It's the grace combining natural ability and uncountable hours of practice. We're awed by such extreme grace, but if our eyes are open, we can see beyond the dance floor. Grace isn't just about how we move. It's about who we are. Handling life with grace means taking a measured approach, not immediately reacting in an emotional way. It's about responding in a balanced manner—even in an awkward situation.

"IN ALL AFFAIRS OF HUMAN LIFE, SOCIAL AS WELL AS POLITICAL, I HAVE REMARKED THAT COURTESIES OF A SMALL AND TRIVIAL CHARACTER ARE THE ONES THAT STRIKE DEEPEST TO THE GRATEFUL AND APPRECIATING HEART."

– UNITED STATES STATESMAN HENRY CLAY

PROFILE IN GRACE:

One of the most striking exhibits at the Abraham Lincoln Presidential Museum and Library in Springfield, Illinois, is an extremely unpleasant area devoted to the terrible things said, written, and drawn about the man widely considered to be one of the greatest leaders in U.S. history. If you think politics today is worse than ever, a walk through this exhibit is an eye-opener. Landing in office with less than 40% of the popular vote and a divided nation, Lincoln couldn't just rely on good decision-making and trusted advisors. He also had to maintain an image of control and grace no matter how bleak things appeared to be. Is it any wonder that Lincoln's sense of humor is one of his most remembered characteristics?

NOBLE

Noble individuals look at themselves rather than others and hold their own behavior to a high standard instead of worrying about others not meeting expectations. To be seen as noble is to be seen as someone principled and trustworthy—not as a means to an end, but as an end unto itself. And it's a trait that is within reach no matter what one's station in life may be.

"THERE IS NOTHING NOBLE IN BEING SUPERIOR TO YOUR FELLOW MEN. TRUE NOBILITY LIES IN BEING SUPERIOR TO YOUR FORMER SELF."

– AUTHOR ERNEST HEMINGWAY

TALENT

There are people who ascribe talent completely to DNA—you're either born with it or you aren't. But while people are predisposed to certain abilities, there has been no instance of anyone being born a great actor, dancer, athlete, or leader. Talent is a combination of what you are born with and what you do with it. Which is why so many artists thank a deity when they accept an award. The spark may have been there from the beginning, but hard work fanned the flame and gave it power.

"TALENT IS A DULL KNIFE THAT WILL CUT NOTHING UNLESS IT IS WIELDED WITH GREAT FORCE."

— AUTHOR STEPHEN KING

PROFILE IN TALENT:

As adept at dramas ("The Emperor Jones," "Othello") as he was in musicals (most famously "Show Boat"), Paul Robeson's acting and musical talent was more than enough for him to be mentioned here. But that was far from the whole show. Robeson was also a first-rate athlete, proving himself on the Rutgers football team and continuing to excel in the NFL . . . all while going to law school. He left school, temporarily, for parts in Broadway shows, but returned to finish his degree. Throughout his career, his involvement in social and civil rights issues put his oratorical skills to positive use. And even after being blacklisted during the McCarthy era, Robeson managed a comeback both as a writer and an acclaimed, in-demand performer.

AMBITION

While it often carries a negative connotation, ambition—when accompanied by attributes such as fairness and empathy—can be enormously positive. It's what helps us strive to achieve and to leave the next generation a better world than the one we found. In a world where there's plenty to hold you back, ambition can be the boost that gets you over hurdles and beyond setbacks. Instead of a bad thing, think of it as keeping your goals in sight and moving toward them—even when the road gets rocky.

TENACITY

Earning a reputation for hard work can be a plus in the workplace, but it should also be a point of personal pride—whether anyone else notices it or not. Yes, hard work can help you achieve much more than you might have otherwise. But lack of success does not mean that someone hasn't worked hard. You'll find lots of so-called ordinary people who work hard to obtain even basic needs.

PROFILE IN TENACITY:

From a political prison to the President of South Africa—and its first black head of state—Nelson Mandela has long been an inspiration to those fighting against oppression. With a long history of political protest, he bravely survived a 27-year prison term, much of it in an 8' x 7' cell with only a straw mat for a bed and a limit of one letter and one visit every six months. Once released, Mandela negotiated an end to apartheid, helped organize elections and, when he won, pushed for reconciliation rather than revenge. Weathering criticism from both the left and the right, he stayed true to his ideals, earning the nickname "Father of the Nation" in his native country.

"BEING BUSY DOES NOT ALWAYS MEAN REAL WORK. THE OBJECT OF ALL WORK IS PRODUCTION OR ACCOMPLISHMENT AND TO EITHER OF THESE ENDS THERE MUST BE FORETHOUGHT, SYSTEM, PLANNING, INTELLIGENCE AND HONEST PURPOSE, AS WELL AS PERSPIRATION."

– INVENTOR THOMAS EDISON

STEADFAST

The word steadfast comes from an Old English word meaning "standing firm." From Sir Thomas More and Joan of Arc to Martin Luther King, history is filled with heroes who stood firm against what they knew to be wrong. Having the courage of your convictions is a powerful trait. And, provided you also have your ears and mind open to other views, it can change the world.

TRUTH

We have access to more information than at any time in human history. Yet somehow the truth seems even harder to pin down. The tidal wave of misinformation, though, should not discourage you from being a seeker of truth. Getting facts straight, understanding context, and being able to weed out the false are now essential skills. And, as the saying goes, the truth shall set you free.

"MOST MEN WOULD RATHER
DENY A HARD TRUTH THAN FACE IT."
– AUTHOR GEORGE R.R. MARTIN IN *A GAME OF THRONES*

PROFILE IN TRUTH:

Standing up for truth is core to the career of James Randi, a magician who found himself appalled by the way tricks of his trade were being used by religious charlatans and alleged psychics to bilk the innocent and gullible. Working undercover and using a team of researchers, he helped expose the way so-called faith healers were taking advantage of people at their most vulnerable, bringing their methods to national attention via popular television shows, books including *Flim-Flam*, and public lectures. "Magicians are the most honest people in the world," said Randi. "They tell you they're gonna fool you, and then they do it." As for the dishonest, Randi's offer of $1 million to anyone who could scientifically prove any claims of the paranormal was not claimed during the 20 years it was available.

→ **IT'S A FACT:** ←

FOR YEARS, THE HONEST TEA COMPANY HAS BEEN PLACING UNMANNED HONOR STATIONS STOCKED WITH ITS PRODUCTS AROUND THE U.S. THE RESULTS SO FAR: A NATIONAL AVERAGE OF 93% HONESTY.

ENCOURAGE

When we fall into a creative, professional, or personal funk, sometimes what gets us through is an encouraging word—something which makes the case for putting one foot in front of the other. Being the kind of person who can provide such encouragement—which includes being sensitive enough to know when and how much encouragement is appropriate—can make a huge difference in someone's life.

→→→ IT'S A FACT: ←←←

A STUDY PUBLISHED IN *AMERICAN BEHAVIORAL SCIENTIST* FOUND THAT
MEMBERS OF TOP PERFORMING BUSINESS TEAMS GAVE EACH OTHER
MORE THAN FIVE POSITIVE COMMENTS FOR EVERY CRITICISM.

"FOR ME, LIFE IS ABOUT
BEING POSITIVE AND HOPEFUL,
CHOOSING TO BE JOYFUL,
CHOOSING TO BE ENCOURAGING,
CHOOSING TO BE EMPOWERING."

– SINGER BILLY PORTER

BEAUTY

Talk about beauty these days and you run the risk of being perceived as shallow. That assumes, though, that you buy into the old saw that beauty is only skin-deep. However, a quick trip through an art museum will reveal how the idea of beauty has changed over the years, and how the true artist recognizes the beauty projecting from within. It's the same with people. Any of us can cite examples of people whose confidence, depth, warmth, and/or style accentuate their natural features in a way that compels attention. While few people today fit the absurd criteria popularized in magazines—with their teams of stylists and airbrushed photography—feeling beautiful and seeing beauty in others is nothing to be ashamed of. Reducing unnecessary self-criticism and seeing yourself as beautiful—as a unique creation— can help you create, and achieve, your goals.

"THE MOST BEAUTIFUL PEOPLE WE HAVE KNOWN ARE THOSE WHO HAVE KNOWN DEFEAT, KNOWN SUFFERING, KNOWN STRUGGLE, KNOWN LOSS, AND HAVE FOUND THEIR WAY OUT OF THE DEPTHS."

– DR. ELISABETH KUBLER-ROSS

"A PERSON WHO HAS GOOD THOUGHTS CANNOT EVER BE UGLY. YOU CAN HAVE A WONKY NOSE AND A CROOKED MOUTH AND A DOUBLE CHIN AND STICK-OUT TEETH, BUT IF YOU HAVE GOOD THOUGHTS THEY WILL SHINE OUT OF YOUR FACE LIKE SUNBEAMS AND YOU WILL ALWAYS LOOK LOVELY."

– AUTHOR ROALD DAHL, *THE TWITS*

89.

SOULFUL

Whether or not you believe in the existence of a soul doesn't mean you can't appreciate soulfulness—or develop your own. Soulfulness comes from a combination of seeing and feeling things deeply, with both thoughtfulness and empathy. A soulful person isn't necessarily the quietest person in the room. Instead, it's a person who comes across as connected to the universe in a special way. And that's usually the person people gravitate to in times of grief or transcendent joy.

There are countless reasons to be negative. Just turn on the news or log on to Twitter and you'll find plenty. But an optimist is far from being simply naïve, and they don't necessarily sport a pair of rose-colored glasses. Instead, they are someone who successfully makes an effort, conscious or not, to see the world as a hopeful place. Note the cancer patient who, after diagnosis, took up the piano. Without optimism, we wouldn't have the scientific achievements we have—nor the pioneering spirit that led so many to seek better lives.

"DO NOT ANTICIPATE TROUBLE, OR WORRY
ABOUT WHAT MAY NEVER HAPPEN.
KEEP IN THE SUNLIGHT."

– BENJAMIN FRANKLIN

PROFILE IN HOPE:

Ask an average American to outline President John F. Kennedy's specific policies and you are likely to be met with blank stares. But ask about his attitude about the future of the country and you'll likely hear the word "optimistic." "The American, by nature, is optimistic," he said. "He is experimental, an inventor and a builder who builds best when called upon to build greatly." In encouraging the country to ask "Why not?" instead of "Why?" Kennedy's optimism helped make public service appealing and pointed the country toward what seemed to be impossible when he first suggested it—a manned moon landing.

ADVENTURE

The adventurous are willing to move away from their comfort zone. That's one of the reasons so much great fiction is built upon a quest of some kind. Taking steps into the unknown is at the very heart of adventure. And that applies both physically and emotionally. While most of us don't have the means to venture into a previously unexplored place on the planet, we can apply for a job with a new company, take on a previously unexplored hobby, or take steps to finally get to know the stranger across the street.

PROFILE IN ADVENTUROUSNESS:

Kristine McDivitt Tompkins, former CEO of Patagonia, and her husband, North Face founder Doug Tompkins, had no shortage of adventures—as you'd suspect from the companies they ran. Dedicated to preserving the wilderness, they experienced it first-hand scaling rocks and paddling down remote rivers around the world. But eventually, they left the grid and moved to Chile and Argentina. They even climbed the Himalayas together. After Doug died in a kayaking accident, Kristine didn't give up on the adventurous life. Instead, she continued working to preserve such lands for others to enjoy. Because of her and her husband's work, their adopted countries now have five new national parks, while other parks have been expanded.

"A FELLOW OF MEDIOCRE TALENT WILL REMAIN A MEDIOCRITY, WHETHER HE TRAVELS OR NOT; BUT ONE OF SUPERIOR TALENT (WHICH WITHOUT IMPIETY I CANNOT DENY THAT I POSSESS) WILL GO TO SEED IF HE ALWAYS REMAINS IN THE SAME PLACE."

– WOLFGANG AMADEUS MOZART

AUTHENTIC

We make judgments not just by what is said, but by how words and actions match up. Is the walk the same as the talk? Does there seem to be a genuine connection between what someone says and what that person does? A big part of life is searching for our own authentic self. And being honest and open-minded about your authentic and inauthentic moments is an important part of anyone's efforts to become a better person.

"THE PRIVILEGE OF A LIFETIME IS
TO BECOME WHO YOU TRULY ARE."
– PSYCHIATRIC PIONEER CARL JUNG

→ ABOUT THE AUTHOR ←

Lou Harry is the author of more than 30 books including *Office Dares, The High-Impact Infidelity Diet; A Novel, Creative Block,* and *Kid Culture.* His writing has appeared in publications ranging from *Men's Health* to *The Sondheim Review.* By day, he serves as Arts & Entertainment Editor for the *Indianapolis Business Journal* (www.ipj.com/arts).

Find him at www.louharry.com or by tweeting @LouHarry.

IF YOU ENJOYED THIS BOOK OR IT HAS TOUCHED YOUR LIFE IN SOME WAY,
WE'D LOVE TO HEAR FROM YOU.

PLEASE WRITE A REVIEW AT HALLMARK.COM,
E-MAIL US AT BOOKNOTES@HALLMARK.COM,
OR SEND YOUR COMMENTS TO:

HALLMARK BOOK FEEDBACK
P.O. BOX 419034
MAIL DROP 100
KANSAS CITY, MO 64141